A YEAR OF
DAILY CALM

A YEAR OF
DAILY CALM

A Guided Journal to Creating
Tranquility Every Day

Kate Hanley

NATIONAL GEOGRAPHIC

WASHINGTON, D.C.

Published by the National Geographic Society
1145 17th Street N.W., Washington, D.C. 20036

Copyright © 2015 National Geographic Society

ISBN: 978-1-4262-1560-5

The National Geographic Society is one of the world's largest nonprofit
scientific and educational organizations. Its mission is to inspire people to
care about the planet. Founded in 1888, the Society is member supported
and offers a community for members to get closer to explorers, connect with
other members, and help make a difference. The Society reaches more than
450 million people worldwide each month through *National Geographic* and other
magazines; National Geographic Channel; television documentaries; music;
radio; films; books; DVDs; maps; exhibitions; live events; school publishing
programs; interactive media; and merchandise. National Geographic has
funded more than 10,000 scientific research, conservation, and exploration
projects and supports an education program promoting geographic literacy.
For more information, visit www.nationalgeographic.com.

National Geographic Society
1145 17th Street N.W.
Washington, D.C. 20036-4688 U.S.A.

Your purchase supports our nonprofit work and makes you part of our global
community. Thank you for sharing our belief in the power of science, exploration, and storytelling to change the world. To activate your member benefits,
complete your free membership profile at natgeo.com/joinnow.

For information about special discounts for bulk purchases, please contact
National Geographic Books Special Sales: ngspecsales@ngs.org

For rights or permissions inquiries, please contact National Geographic Books
Subsidiary Rights: ngbookrights@ngs.org

Interior design by Katie Olsen/Melissa Farris

Printed in Hong Kong
15/THK/1

CONTENTS

INTRODUCTION

A CULTURAL CATCHPHRASE in the late 1990s, "Serenity now!" still resonates today—and not just because of the brilliance of *Seinfeld*. We all want to feel calmer, and we'd like it to happen immediately, thank you very much!

Unfortunately, there's no incantation we can chant to summon instant peace. Our minds naturally fluctuate; our experience of tranquility is typically fleeting.

So how can we keep calm on a daily basis? Consider the words of Buddhist teacher Thich Nhat Hanh, "Peace is every step." Just like walking, calm requires action. It requires consistency. And even if it should come naturally to everyone, it takes practice to perfect. You may occasionally need guidance to find your way, but that's what this book is for.

I know from experience that inner calm doesn't come easily. After I had two children in two years, I was overwhelmed and anxiety-ridden at the thought of keeping these two creatures alive. So I gave up my 15-year yoga and meditation practice, thinking I was doing myself a favor by shortening my to-do list.

That, naturally, was when things really went off the rails.

I turned to food and wine for comfort. That led to weight gain and impaired sleep, which made me cranky and down on myself—and that, in turn, made me more inclined to pick fights with my husband and obsess over small things that didn't really matter in an attempt to make myself feel better.

The key to getting out of my tough spot turned out to be the techniques included in this book: simple, quick practices that help you breathe a little deeper and slow down enough to access your own well of inner calm.

Whether you're in crisis mode or not, this book is designed to meet you right where you are. Every exercise has been selected to help you shed some burden and lift your spirits. Every page offers a chance to pause and reflect. Add them up over the course of a year, and you've got a big shift in perspective that comes in easy, digestible bites.

Here are a few ways to incorporate this journal into your life with as much success, and as little stress, as possible:

- **Consider it a (very inexpensive) therapist.** This journal is your opportunity to get important thoughts, beliefs, and ideas out of your head and onto the page. Reading back over your words gives your conscious mind the chance to process— and get on board with—the things your subconscious is

yearning for. Once you do, you no longer have to carry it all around with you, creating space in your mind for deeper calm and contentment.

- **Make it an integral part of your maintenance plan for inner calm.** Perhaps you've never had a strategy for relaxation and reflection before, but you do now: You're holding it in your hands. Whenever you need a moment of quiet, or want to invite an insight to come and land on your shoulder, this is your place to turn. It will turn down the volume of your stressful thoughts and amplify your inner wisdom.

- **Make it something you co-author.** This book is rare because it's incomplete upon publication. *You* are the one person in the world who can make it whole. Fill it with doodles, deep thoughts, the first things that pop into your head—whatever you add will be perfect. Enjoy this chance to be unedited.

- **Use it as a chance to deepen a relationship.**
Buy a copy for a friend and ask her to join you
on this journey. When you share insights and cel-
ebrations with each other ("I explained how I was
feeling to the kids instead of yelling at them!"),
you inspire one another and you give power to
those new seeds sprouting tendrils in your mind.

- **Use it as an opportunity to learn there is no
such thing as "too late."** Don't worry if you forget
about filling in this journal for a few weeks; you
can pick up where you left off or skip what you
missed. Jump around or go through one day at a
time. The only pace you need to commit to is the
one that feels good to you.

Above all, view this book as an invitation to make
changes that speak to your soul. Make them with a
light, loving touch—no stressing or striving! Here's to
discovering your own pace, and to knowing how to create inner and outer peace anytime, anywhere.

• • •

January

Transition

JANUARY 1

TRANSITION TIP
Look Ahead

Change—even good change—can overwhelm.
To help you stay steady and motivated, take a
moment now to think about what you'd like
to do differently: How many minutes per day
or per week will you dedicate to cultivating
a sense of calm? What will you do less of
to open up space in your schedule?

Once you can *really* visualize how a change
will integrate into your daily life, your odds
of success will increase.

• • •

JANUARY 2–3

There will come a time when
you believe everything is finished.
That will be the beginning.

~ LOUIS L'AMOUR

JANUARY 4–5

Faith is taking the first step
when you don't see the whole staircase.

~ MARTIN LUTHER KING, JR.

....
....
....
....
....
....
....

JANUARY 6

THINK ABOUT...
Soothing Your Soul

Write down ten activities that steady you.
They can be quick (a deep breath, a sigh,
a stretch) or a little more time-intensive
(a walk with the dog, an afternoon in the
garden, a cup of tea).

Whatever activities you list, be sure they
actually help you feel like all is right with
the world. Avoid adding things that only *seem*
like they soothe. If yoga class makes you feel
insecure about your flexibility, for example,
then leave it off the list!

• • •

JANUARY 7

TRY THIS
Get Trigger Happy

We all get our buttons pushed. Perhaps it's
the way your spouse wipes the counter
(or doesn't), or when someone cuts you off
in traffic, or the sight of your boss's name
in your email inbox. In the space below,
name the things that push your buttons.

Let these triggers remind you to do something
calming today—a yoga pose, a silent scream,
or something from the list of soothing activities
you created on January 6. Remember, while you
can't control what happens to you, you can
control how you react. Choose to respond
from a place of peace and watch magic happen.

• • •

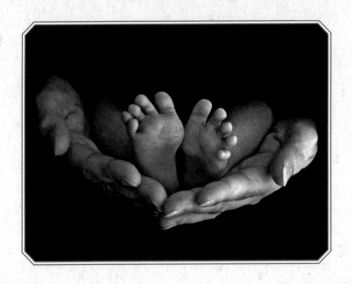

JANUARY 8–9

We are not yet what we shall be,
but we are growing toward it,
the process is not yet finished . . .
~ MARTIN LUTHER

JANUARY 10–11

One doesn't discover new lands without
consenting to lose sight of the shore
for a very long time.

~ ANDRÉ GIDE

January 12

TRANSITION TIP
Bless This Mess

Household chores may seem like unpleasant
tasks, but they can be a steadying force,
especially during times of transition.
Tonight as you load the dishwasher (or brush
your teeth, or fold the laundry), tune in
to your senses. Paying attention to your physical
experience gives your mind space to rest.

If you're doing dishes, notice the feeling
of water on your hands, the sounds
of silverware swishing in the sink, the scent
of your dish soap. Whenever your focus strays,
redirect your thoughts back to the task
at hand. Once done, you'll have more
than a tidy kitchen; you'll have a clear head.

• • •

JANUARY 13

THINK ABOUT . . .
Taking a Breath

Many people say they want to "be more Zen."
But that doesn't mean you should never
get riled—you're human, after all.

Instead, think of being calm as the ability
to reflect before you react. When you give
yourself a moment to take three deep breaths
or slowly count to ten in your head,
you create the opportunity for your body
to calm down and your mind to comprehend
before you engage with the drama du jour.
Coming from a place of peace guarantees
a more pleasing outcome.

• • •

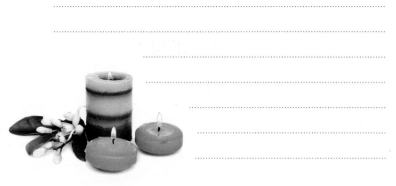

JANUARY 14–15

*An infinite question is often destroyed
by finite answers. To define everything
is to annihilate much that gives us
laughter and joy.*
~ MADELEINE L'ENGLE

....
....
....
....
....
....

JANUARY 16–17

To reach the port of heaven, we must sail sometimes
with the wind and sometimes against it—
but we must sail, and not drift, nor lie at anchor.
~ OLIVER WENDELL HOLMES, SR.

JANUARY 18

TRANSITION TIP
Make Space for Peace

You don't need a pristine house to live
a calmer life, but having a dedicated
soothing spot certainly helps. Find a place
at home where you love to spend time:
a cozy chair by the window, a sunny corner
of your bedroom, the bathtub. Tidy up just this
one spot and add a few things that beckon you
to spend time there—perhaps a candle
and a beautiful painting. Now, whenever you
sense your stress levels rising, you'll know
just where to go to reflect and restore.

• • •

January 19

TRY THIS
Catch Your Zzz's

Sleep too little and your stress rises.
Stress too much and your sleep suffers.
Bust this loop and invite deeper rest with
a nightly wind-down ritual: Turn off all digital
devices and enjoy a few minutes of stretching
or lying in savasana before brushing your teeth.
Below, sketch out your ideal—yet still realistic—
bedtime routine. Tonight, do *just one piece* of this
best-case scenario: Small, consistent steps
are how lasting changes are made.

BONUS TIP: To shift attention away from your
thoughts and into your body as you drift off,
place one hand on your heart and the other
just below your ribs. After a few minutes,
bring the top hand to your lower belly.

• • •

JANUARY 20–21

If the fish had stuck to its gills there would
have been no movement up to the land.
~ CYNTHIA OZICK

....
....
....
....
....
....
....

JANUARY 22–23

Every intersection in the road of life
is an opportunity to make a decision,
and at some I had only to listen.

~ DUKE ELLINGTON

JANUARY 24

THINK ABOUT . . .
Trusting Your Gut

Indecision is a subtle form of self-torture—
you stay stuck as you look for the flaws
in each option. Today, remember a time
when you based a decision only on what you
knew to be true in your bones. How did it feel?
How did the decision change
the course of your life?

Use this memory to remind yourself that deep
down you always know the next best step,
and allow it to help you make choices
from a place of wisdom.

• • •

JANUARY 25–26

Our way is not soft grass, it's a mountain path with lots of rocks. But it goes upwards, forward, toward the sun.

~ RUTH WESTHEIMER

JANUARY 27–28

As time passes we all get better
at blazing a trail
through the thicket of advice.

~ MARGOT BENNETT

JANUARY 29–30

If we don't change, we don't grow.
If we don't grow, we are not really living.

~ GAIL SHEEHY

....
....
....
....
....
....
....

JANUARY 31

TRY THIS
Invite Stillness

Many ancient traditions like yoga and martial
arts consider earth a source of stability
and energy, yet we spend most of our time
hovering above it—sitting on chairs or lying
in beds. Today, connect to the ground by
lying on your back in a simple savasana:
legs out straight, arms at your sides,
head relaxed. Close your eyes and melt
into the floor like a pat of butter on a stack
of pancakes. Stay in this position
for at least five minutes.

Call on the memory of this profound sense
of calm to ground you later as you move
through your day.

• • •

FEBRUARY

Joy

FEBRUARY 1

JOY TIP
Find Your Happy Place

Joy may feel light and bubbly, but this emotional
powerhouse also has the capacity to evaporate
sadness, anger, and despair. To invite more joy
into your life, follow these steps inspired
by Buddhist nun Pema Chödrön:

Sitting quietly, recall a time when your heart
swelled with happiness. Relive every sensory
detail you can muster. Imagine the good
feelings evoked by that memory permeating
through your every cell.

Remember, this internal well of joy resides
within you. It may feel buried at times,
but the more you practice accessing it,
the more it will grow.

• • •

FEBRUARY 2–3

Where there is joy there is creation.

~ HINDU SCRIPTURE

FEBRUARY 4–5

*Thousands of candles can be lighted
from a single candle, and the life
of the candle will not be shortened.
Happiness never decreases by being shared.*

~ BUDDHA

FEBRUARY 6

TRY THIS
Let Yourself off the Hook

Any incident from your past that
makes you wince is like an invisible basketball
shackled to your ankle. It doesn't seem
like a big deal until you think about
all the little ways that ball trips you up.

Clear your mental slate by writing down
the answers to these questions:
What do you judge yourself for?
What do you forgive yourself for?

Let today be the day you start untying
those old knots.

• • •

....
....
....
....
....
....
....
....

FEBRUARY 7–8

*Against the assault of laughter
nothing can stand.*

~ MARK TWAIN

....

....

....

....

....

....

FEBRUARY 9–10

*Friendship improves happiness
and abates misery, by the doubling
of our joy and the dividing of our grief.*
~ MARCUS TULLIUS CICERO

FEBRUARY 11–12

*Most folks are about as happy
as they make up their minds to be.*

~ ABRAHAM LINCOLN

....
....
....
....
....
....
....
....

FEBRUARY 13

THINK ABOUT . . .
Happy Surroundings

So far this month, we've addressed how
to make your inner environment more joyful.
Your outer environment—including the people
you see regularly—is just as important. Why?
Like smoking and obesity, happiness tends
to run in groups.

How happy are the people with whom you spend
the most time? If the answer is "not very"
or "not enough," how can you seek out—
or create—a more joyful crowd?

• • •

FEBRUARY 14

JOY TIP
Embrace Meditation

Research shows regular meditators have higher levels of dopamine and serotonin—neurotransmitters associated with pleasure and resilience. The key word in that last sentence is *regular:* Consistency counts.

To start your meditation practice, set your intention below. How often will you meditate each day? For how long? When? Write out your plan and consider it a promise to yourself.

Here's a basic technique:
In a quiet place, sit comfortably with a straight spine. Close your eyes and begin silently counting each time you exhale. When you get to ten, start at one again.

• • •

FEBRUARY 15–16

*The supreme happiness of life
is the conviction of being loved for yourself,
or, more correctly speaking,
loved in spite of yourself.*

~ VICTOR HUGO

....
....
....
....
....
....

FEBRUARY 17–18

The essence of pleasure is spontaneity.
~ GERMAINE GREER

FEBRUARY 19

TRY THIS
Say Yes to You

What do you do for fun? Try a new restaurant?
Call in sick and read a book? Meet your sweetie
for a quickie at lunch? Write your list
on the lines below, and let the simple act
of writing them down be all the permission
you need to make them a reality. The more
you take on a proactive role in courting
simple pleasures, the more joy will find you.

• • •

FEBRUARY 20

THINK ABOUT . . .
Open the Door to Happiness

So many of us feel that to want joy is
frivolous, or greedy, or even foolish.
To see the limiting beliefs that might be
keeping you from allowing more happiness
into your life, answer these questions:

As a kid, I got the message that happiness
was ....

When I see unabashedly happy people,
I think ....

Committing your answers to paper will reveal
the walls you may have put up against joy.
The very act of observing those thoughts
will help you transform them.

• • •

FEBRUARY 21–22

*We're so engaged in doing things to achieve purposes
of outer value that we forget that the inner value,
the rapture that is associated with being alive,
is what it's all about.*

~ JOSEPH CAMPBELL

FEBRUARY 23–24

*Peace is joy at rest, and joy
is peace on its feet.*
~ ANNE LAMOTT

FEBRUARY 25–26

A merry heart doeth good like a medicine.

~ PROVERBS 17:22

....

....

....

....

....

....

....

....

FEBRUARY 27

JOY TIP
The Golden Rule

A paradox of joy is that doing nice things for
others makes *you* feel good. What simple things
can you do to increase another's happiness?
This isn't about overextending yourself.
It's about building on something you're already
doing: inviting a playmate along on your next
family outing (the kids, and the playmate's
parents, will thank you), doubling a batch
of chili and delivering leftovers to someone
in need, or paying an unexpected compliment
in an otherwise standard email exchange.
The minimal added effort will come back
to you in a wave of good feelings.

Remember, anytime joy feels inaccessible
you can court it by simply doing something nice
for someone else. It's that simple—
and that miraculous.

• • •

FEBRUARY 28–29

*Mirth is like a flash of lightning,
that breaks through a gloom of clouds,
and glitters for a moment; cheerfulness keeps
up a kind of daylight in the mind, and fills it
with a steady and perpetual serenity.*

~ JOSEPH ADDISON

....

....

....

....

....

March

Experience

MARCH 1

EXPERIENCE TIP
Making Time

We all have things we long to do but rarely get
around to—such as meditate, exercise, catch up
with friends, or write a novel. It's easy to say,
"I don't have time for that," yet each
of us has the same 168 hours each week.
That's no mere morsel; it's a heaping helping.
"I don't have time" is simply untrue.

Starting today, use this phrase instead:
"That's not a priority for me." It will help
you see how you've been subtly talking yourself
out of those important pursuits before
you even begin. Watch how that insight
empowers you to make wiser choices.

• • •

MARCH 2–3

It is a mistake to regard age as a downhill grade
toward dissolution. The reverse is true.
As one grows older, one climbs with surprising strides.

~ GEORGE SAND

....

....

....

....

....

....

MARCH 4–5

*Growth and self-transformation
cannot be delegated.*

~ LEWIS MUMFORD

MARCH 6–7

Try new recipes, learn from your mistakes,
be fearless, and above all have fun.

~ JULIA CHILD

MARCH 8

TRY THIS
Wipe the Slate Clean

Unpleasant feelings—stress, the blues,
or just plain angst—can morph into bigger
woes if they remain unaddressed.
Get to the root of your feelings by listing
everything you're worried about.

Then ask yourself: What one or two traits
will help me deal with these issues?
Possibilities include openness, bravery, honesty,
flexibility, love, or gentleness. Orient your
attention toward the antidote instead
of the problem, and watch those concerns
disperse like a pile of leaves on a windy day.

• • •

MARCH 9–10

The easiest way to avoid wrong notes
is to never open your mouth and sing.
What a mistake that would be.

~ JOAN OLIVER GOLDSMITH

MARCH 11–12

We know too much and feel too little.

~ BERTRAND RUSSELL

MARCH 13–14

Every beginning is only a sequel,
after all, and the book of events
is always open halfway through.

~ WISŁAWA SZYMBORSKA

March 15

THINK ABOUT...
The Power of Progress

Three months into your year of daily calm,
take a moment to think about what has shifted.
Do you respond to stressful events differently?
Has focusing more on positive emotions
changed your day-to-day experience?
What benefits have you gained?

Tiny steps lead to big changes.
Let the progress you've already made
inspire you to keep going.

• • •

MARCH 16–17

*Our strength is often composed of the weakness
we're damned if we're going to show.*

~ MIGNON MCLAUGHLIN

MARCH 18–19

People are like bicycles. They can keep their balance only as long as they keep moving.

~ ALBERT EINSTEIN

MARCH 20

TRY THIS
Listen Carefully

Researchers have found that mechanical noises—
jackhammers, trucks idling, or brakes
screeching—are some of the most disturbing
sounds to human ears. Today, seek out
genuinely calming surroundings—the nearest
woods, a library, or even your own backyard—
and listen carefully. This new focus
will ease your mind, and the thoughtful break
from activity will refresh your spirit.

• • •

MARCH 21–22

*If facts are the seeds that later produce
knowledge or wisdom, then the emotions
and the impressions of the senses are
the fertile soil in which the seeds must grow.*

~ RACHEL CARSON

of your life,

N

MARCH 23–24

You practice and you get better.
It's very simple.
~ PHILIP GLASS

MARCH 25–26

*Nothing ever becomes real
till it is experienced.*

~ JOHN KEATS

MARCH 28

*Above all, be the heroine
not the victim*

~ NORA EPHRON

MARCH 30–31

You won't win until you learn how to lose.

~ KAREEM ABDUL-JABBAR

APRIL

❦

Simplicity

APRIL 1

SIMPLICITY TIP
Prioritize You

If you don't have an overall sense of your
larger goals, you'll likely focus on only what's
time-sensitive and neglect important things
that have indefinite deadlines.

Take a moment to write down one or two main
areas of focus for you right now, whether it's
your health, home, work, relationship, or kids.
Then brainstorm a few simple ways to
significantly improve each of your targeted areas.
During the next week, do one or two of these
things each day before you do anything else.
You'll also rest easier knowing you're
tending to things that matter.

• • •

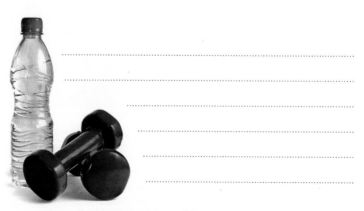

APRIL 2–3

So simplify the problem of life, distinguish the necessary and the real. Probe the earth to see where your main roots run.

~ HENRY DAVID THOREAU

....
....
....
....
....
....

April 4–5

Let silence take you to the core of life.

~ Rumi

....

....

....

....

....

....

....

....

APRIL 6

SIMPLICITY TIP
Create Downtime

You plan for productivity at work, but if you lack a basic schedule for your free time, it's all too likely you'll fill it with the equivalent of empty calories.

In the lines below, plan out an ideal week. When would you exercise, read, pursue a hobby, and spend quality time with friends and family? This may take some trial and error to get exactly right, but planning when you'll do the things that most sustain you will increase the likelihood that you'll actually do them.

• • •

APRIL 7–8

Sometimes the most important thing
in a whole day is the rest we take
between two deep breaths.

~ ETTY HILLESUM

APRIL 9–10

*Making the simple complicated
is commonplace; making the complicated simple,
awesomely simple, that's creativity.*

~ CHARLES MINGUS

April 11–12

Do what you can, with what you have,
where you are.

~ Theodore Roosevelt

APRIL 13–14

Omit needless words.

~ WILLIAM STRUNK, JR., AND E. B. WHITE

....

....

....

....

....

....

....

....

APRIL 15

THINK ABOUT . . .
The Best Intentions

For any task on which you're about to embark—
like cooking dinner, for instance—ask yourself,
What's my intention? To do something creative?
To spend time with friends or family?
Or merely to fuel up? There are no right
answers, but clarifying *why* you're doing
whatever it is you're about to do will help focus
your attention and streamline your efforts.
The result? Less stress and bigger impact.

• • •

APRIL 16–17

It is the sweet, simple things of life
which are the real ones after all.

~ LAURA INGALLS WILDER

APRIL 18–19

*Joy in looking and comprehending
is nature's most beautiful gift.*

~ ALBERT EINSTEIN

APRIL 20

TRY THIS
Call It Like You Feel It

The next time you're feeling off,
challenge yourself to resist the urge to blame
or complain. Instead, name the emotion
you're experiencing.
To practice, fill in the following blanks:

I'm feeling .... because

....

You may have to write the sentence
a few times to arrive at the truth, but the
detective work is worthwhile: Acknowledging
a negative feeling frees you from it
and helps to transform it.

• • •

....

....

....

....

....

....

....

APRIL 21–22

Simplicity is the keynote of all true elegance.
~ COCO CHANEL

APRIL 23–24

Believe that you have it, and you have it.

~ LATIN PROVERB

APRIL 25–26

The wisdom of life consists
in the elimination of non-essentials.
~ LIN YUTANG

APRIL 27

THINK ABOUT . . .
What's in It for You?

Think back on the last week and recall
when you spent too much time and effort
for too little payoff—the unappreciative client
you bent over backward for, the meal you cooked
that your kids wouldn't touch, the marathon call
with a friend that left you feeling unheard.
Then see if you can find a common theme.
Were you trying to avoid mistakes?
Keep the peace? Live up to some ideal?
Seeing the patterns of how and why
you try too hard can help you choose
a simpler path in the future.

• • •

APRIL 28

SIMPLICITY TIP
Ignite Your Superpowers

Each of us has a unique set of skills such
as a knack for metaphor, the ability to read
a situation and know exactly what must be done,
or a gift for seeing the positive. These traits
come so easily that you forget to value them—
or even to recognize them. *But they're your best stuff!*

What comes naturally to you? Write down your
one-of-a-kind skills below and think about how
you can incorporate them more in your work,
your relationships, and your life. Tapping into
these innate talents makes the complicated work
of personal growth simpler and more fulfilling.

• • •

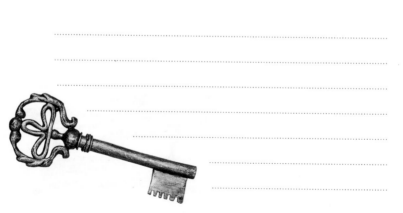

APRIL 29–30

*Learn to wish that everything
may happen as it does.*

~ Epictetus

MAY

Mindfulness

MAY 1

MINDFULNESS TIP
You've Done This Before

It's tempting to think of mindfulness—
paying attention, thinking nonjudgmentally—
as something exotic. But you've probably
experienced mindfulness already,
even if you've never formally tried it.
Mindfulness happens anytime you focus on a
task so much that you think about nothing else,
like the time you stayed up late cleaning after
you got bit by the decluttering bug.

Ask yourself: What activities inspire a state
of relaxed concentration? How can you bring
that experience to tasks where you tend
to zone out?

• • •

MAY 2–3

Let us not look back in anger,
nor forward in fear,
but around us in awareness.

~ JAMES THURBER

MAY 4–5

*The mind is its own place, and in itself
can make a Heaven of Hell, a Hell of Heaven.*

~ JOHN MILTON

MAY 6–7

*Little by little, through patience
and repeated effort, the mind will
become stilled in the Self.*

~ HINDU SCRIPTURE

....
....
....
....

MAY 8

THINK ABOUT . . .
Redirecting (Instead of Reprimanding)

Mindfulness isn't not thinking; it's noticing
when your mind wanders and simply
guiding it back to what's happening now.
Today, whenever you notice your attention has
drifted, resist the urge to think unkind thoughts
(à la, "Pay attention, space cadet!").
Instead, talk to yourself with kindness:
"Just try again" or "You can do this."
Adjusting your attitude reduces angst
and empowers you to entertain—
and pursue—new possibilities.

• • •

MAY 9–10

Happiness, not in another place but this place . . .
not for another hour, but this hour.
~ WALT WHITMAN

MAY 11–12

Remember, remember,
this is now, and now, and now.
Live it, feel it, cling to it.

~ SYLVIA PLATH

....

....

....

....

....

....

MAY 13–14

*Learning to live in the present moment
is part of the path of joy.*

~ SARAH BAN BREATHNACH

....
....
....
....
....
....
....
....

MAY 15

TRY THIS
Find Your Feet

Being mindful may seem easy in theory,
but it's a different story when you're out
in the world. Whenever you find your attention pulled in multiple directions, ask yourself,
Where are my feet? If they aren't both flat
on the floor, put them there. If they are,
imagine they had roots reaching deep into
the ground. This simple physical focus
will invite your mind to pay attention to where
you are and what's happening right now.

• • •

MAY 16–17

*Strange as it may seem today to say,
the aim of life is to live, and to live means
to be aware, joyously, drunkenly,
serenely, divinely aware.*

~ HENRY MILLER

MAY 18–19

*Being is sufficient. Being is all. The cheerful,
sunny self you are missing will return,
as it always does, but only being will bring it back.*

~ ALICE WALKER

....

....

....

....

....

....

MAY 20–21

Our true nature is not some deal that we have to live up to. It's who we are right now, and that's what we can make friends with and celebrate.

~ PEMA CHÖDRÖN

MAY 22

MINDFULNESS TIP
Stop Squeezing Things In

If you're constantly running late, you are
spending the majority of your time anticipating
what's next instead of paying attention to what's
happening now—a pervasive source of stress.

Brainstorm ways to create a distinct boundary
between each task: Schedule a ten-minute
buffer between meetings, get up a bit earlier
to avoid starting the day behind, or opt
to stay put during a pocket of downtime
instead of running errands. You may end up
doing less, but the mental energy you'll save
will help you make each effort your best.

• • •

May 23–24

*Beauty and grace are performed whether
or not we will or sense them.
The least we can do is try to be there.*

~ Annie Dillard

MAY 25–26

Listening to the birds can be a meditation
if you listen with awareness.

~ OSHO

MAY 27

TRY THIS
Take the Day Off

While it's helpful to devote small pockets of time
to mindfulness, dedicating a longer stretch
is a game changer—a true reboot for your mind
and spirit. Look at your calendar and ask:
When can I spend a day (or a few hours)
acting deliberately?

You can still get things done—do the laundry,
make dinner, go for a walk, take a bath—
but the simpler you keep your schedule,
the better, since your goal is absorption.
No planning, no rehashing . . . simply *be*
and watch the insights flow in.

• • •

MAY 28–29

When words become unclear, I shall focus with photographs. When images become inadequate, I shall be content with silence.

~ ANSEL ADAMS

MAY 30–31

*Learn to be quiet enough to hear the sound
of the genuine within yourself so that
you can hear it in other people.*

~ MARIAN WRIGHT EDELMAN

JUNE

❧

Compassion

JUNE 1

COMPASSION TIP
Rejigger Your Worry

While it may stem from concern,
worrying about someone you love may only
make you both feel worse. To truly support
someone, try this mantra from acclaimed
meditation teacher Sharon Salzberg:

Sitting quietly, picture the person's face
in your mind. Then spend a few
minutes repeating silently:

May you be happy.

May you be healthy.

May you be peaceful.

The warm feelings that result from this practice
will overcome any fear you've been feeling—
a positive and uplifting experience
for you both.

• • •

....

....

....

JUNE 2–3

What do we live for, if it is not to make life less difficult for each other?

~ GEORGE ELIOT

....

....

....

....

....

....

June 4–5

*There is no charm equal
to tenderness of heart.*

~ Jane Austen

....
....
....
....
....
....
....

JUNE 6–7

*Sometimes people say unkind
or thoughtless things, and when they do,
it is best to be a little hard of hearing.*

~ RUTH BADER GINSBURG

JUNE 8

COMPASSION TIP
Soften Your Heart

Send some love to your heart with this
restorative yoga pose:

Place a rolled up bath towel or yoga mat
on the floor. Lie down, draping your back
over the roll—which should be perpendicular
to your spine—making your heart the highest
part of your body. (If the tops of your shoulders
don't reach the floor, make a thinner roll.)
Remain in this position for a few minutes,
resting your hands on the floor alongside you,
and imagine gravity and your breath gently
creating more space around your heart.
The opening deepens your breathing and eases
muscular tension in the upper chest,
both of which foster calm.

• • •

JUNE 9–10

The softest thing in the universe
overcomes the hardest.

~ LAO-TZU

....
....
....
....
....
....
....

JUNE 11–12

Let your love be like the misty rains,
coming softly, but flooding the river.

~ MALAGASY PROVERB

....
....
....
....
....
....
....

JUNE 13–14

The greatest good you can do for another
is not just to share your riches
but to reveal to him his own.

~ BENJAMIN DISRAELI

JUNE 15

THINK ABOUT . . .
Keep Your Distance

Think of a difficult person in your life.
Ask yourself if spending time around this
person causes one or both of you to suffer.
Sometimes, the most compassionate thing you
can do for everyone involved is to take a break
from the relationship. Let it be an act of love,
rather than a punishment or power play.
During the separation, use the meditation
from June 1 to project compassion—and don't
be surprised if you come back together
in a much better place down the road.

• • •

JUNE 16–17

*Compassion will cure more sins
than condemnation.*

~ HENRY WARD BEECHER

....

....

....

....

....

....

....

JUNE 18–19

From what we get, we can make a living;
what we give, however, makes a life.

~ ARTHUR ASHE

JUNE 20

THINK ABOUT . . .
Compassion Is an Inside Job

The most important person to offer compassion
to is you. Yes, you! Why? When you allow
yourself to really feel and then take steps
to reduce your own suffering, two things
happen: You are better able to be of service,
and you become a role model to others.

What could you do to alleviate angst in your
own life? Find a quieter apartment? Fire your
worst client? Apologize for a mistake that's been
haunting you? Let the knowledge that your
efforts will ripple out to others inspire
you to get started.

· · ·

JUNE 21–22

*One kind word can warm
three winter months.*

~ JAPANESE PROVERB

JUNE 23–24

When you are good to others,
you are best to yourself.
~ BENJAMIN FRANKLIN

June 25–26

The more one judges,
the less one loves.

~ Honoré de Balzac

JUNE 27

COMPASSION TIP
There Goes the Judge

It's so much easier to judge a foible you see
in someone else than to acknowledge the same
fault in yourself. Think of a person or situation
that's driving you crazy—your daughter's
changing her major *again*, your husband's
dragging his feet on a project, your friend's *still*
complaining about her job but doing little
about it. Instead of fretting over their actions,
ask yourself: How am I perpetuating my own
misery and what can I do about it? Recognizing
and addressing your own issues will help you
have more compassion for your loved one's
predicament and boost your mood. When you're
in a happier, more understanding place,
your odds of being helpful are infinitely higher.

. . .

JUNE 28

TRY THIS
Ask the Right Questions

Identifying with someone else's feelings
requires truly listening and resisting the urge
to fix. The next time someone comes to you
with an issue, challenge yourself to hone in
on her experience. Some phrases that help:

Tell me more about that.

What was that like?

How did that feel?

I understand why you were feeling ....
(use some of her own words).

The connection you'll create will strengthen
the bond between the two of you
and shift both your moods.

• • •

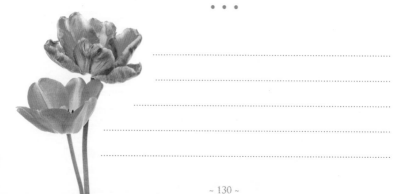

June 29–30

*One's life has value so long as one attributes
value to the lives of others, by means of love,
friendship, indignation and compassion.*

~ Simone de Beauvoir

JULY

Perspective

JULY 1

PERSPECTIVE TIP
Think Like an Explorer

Travel is a great way to see the world through
a new lens, but you don't have to wait for
your next vacation to broaden your perspective.
Challenge yourself to explore your own
environs—take a different route to work, walk
down new-to-you blocks, or sit on the floor
instead of the couch. Seeking out novelty in
your everyday life will strengthen your curiosity,
which studies have associated with emotional
well-being, intelligence, and longevity.

• • •

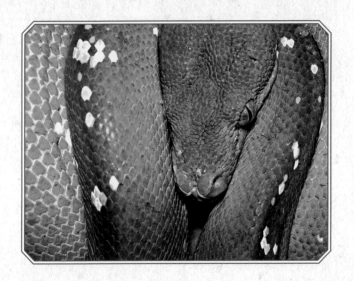

July 2–3

The snake that cannot cast its skin perishes.
So too with those minds which are prevented
from changing their views: they cease to be minds.
~ **Friedrich Nietzsche**

July 4–5

People from a planet without flowers
would think we must be mad with joy
the whole time to have such things about us.

~ Iris Murdoch

....

....

....

....

....

....

We shall not cease from exploration
And the end of all our exploring
Will be to arrive where we started
And know the place for the first time.
~ T. S. ELIOT

....
....
....
....
....
....

JULY 8

TRY THIS
Let It Go

What bad experience do you keep reliving?
An awkward conversation?
The tiff you're having with your neighbor?
A task you've neglected? Free yourself
from whatever's plaguing you by imagining
it's contained within a balloon on a string
that you hold. Envision yourself opening
your hand and watching the balloon drift up
and out of sight. Do it with the intention
of clearing space in your mind to make room
for new solutions to arise.

• • •

JULY 9–10

Better keep yourself clean and bright;
you are the window through which
you must see the world.
~ GEORGE BERNARD SHAW

July 11–12

We are all in the gutter,
but some of us are looking at the stars.
~ Oscar Wilde

....
....
....
....
....
....
....

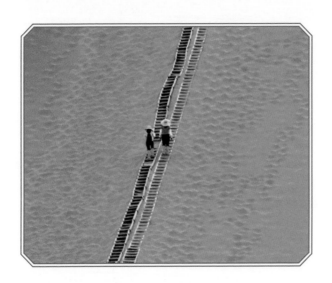

July 13–14

It isn't the mountains ahead that wear you out,
it's the grain of sand in your shoe.

~ Anonymous

JULY 15

PERSPECTIVE TIP
Quit Complaining

We all know how tempting it is to kvetch
about what's bugging us. But research shows
that complaining only reduces your energy
and places your attention on the negative,
a recipe for feeling low and powerless.
For the next three days, dare yourself
not to grumble (even internally!). It will be
a challenge, since our brains are wired
to notice what goes wrong. But refraining
from complaining will force your brain
to find something else—either neutral
or positive—to focus on, which will produce
a palpable boost in mood.

• • •

JULY 16–17

*For us believing physicists, the distinction
between past, present, and future
is only an illusion, even if a stubborn one.*

~ ALBERT EINSTEIN

JULY 18–19

*The voyage of discovery is not in seeking
new landscapes, but in having new eyes.*

~ MARCEL PROUST

....
....
....
....
....
....
....

July 20–21

One can never read the same book twice.

~ Edmund Wilson

....
....
....
....
....
....
....
....

JULY 22

PERSPECTIVE TIP
Change the Station

Music can make a beeline to your heart—
studies have even found that your heart rate
can sync to the beat of a song. Listening to an
uplifting tune can be one of the quickest ways
to shift perspective. What songs make you feel
like anything is possible? Jot down your top
mood-lifting melodies below, then go turn them
into a playlist. You'll never be more than
one button-push away from feeling better.

• • •

JULY 23–24

Imagination is the highest kite that can fly.

~ LAUREN BACALL

July 25–26

Anyone who keeps the ability
to see beauty never grows old.

~ Franz Kafka

JULY 27–28

Some people could look at a mud-puddle and see an ocean with ships.

~ ZORA NEALE HURSTON

JULY 29

THINK ABOUT . . .
Predict Your Own Future

We are so trained to solve problems
and think critically that we often forget
to look for the opportunities in every situation.
Think of something that's got you feeling
stymied or stuck. Now imagine five years
have passed. Ask yourself what lesson or positive
development made it possible for you to resolve
this particular situation. Taking a longer view
will help you see your dilemma with new eyes.

• • •

JULY 30–31

To be seventy years young is sometimes
far more cheerful and hopeful
than to be forty years old.

~ OLIVER WENDELL HOLMES, SR.

AUGUST

Patience

AUGUST 1

PATIENCE TIP
Put on the Brakes

The faster we move through life,
the more turbulence trails along behind us.
Because we're so often in a rush, anything
that slows us down triggers a wave of irritation.
Take away that urgency, and you also
take away a major source of impatience.

In the space below, brainstorm ways you can
slow down. Can you streamline your morning
routine? Delegate one task a day so you have
more space between activities? The capacity for
patience rests within you—but you have to create
space for it to blossom.

• • •

AUGUST 2–3

*Just when the caterpillar
thought the world was over,
it became a butterfly.*

~ ENGLISH PROVERB

....

....

....

....

....

....

AUGUST 4–5

The best way out is always through.

~ ROBERT FROST

....
....
....
....
....
....
....
....
....

AUGUST 6–7

Experience has taught me this,
that we undo ourselves by impatience.
Misfortunes have their life and their limits,
their sickness and their health.

~ MICHEL DE MONTAIGNE

AUGUST 8

THINK ABOUT . . .
Patience Means More Than Waiting

Yes, patience is a virtue. But if you continue
to wait for circumstances to change of their
own accord, you could be waiting a long time—
thus prolonging the misery of limbo.

Think of a situation you'd like to change.
Ask yourself, What action can I take now
to resolve this situation? Understanding that
you can make a difference (no matter how small)
will empower you with an immensely effective
change agent: momentum.

• • •

AUGUST 9–10

Patience, n. a minor form of despair,
disguised as a virtue.

~ AMBROSE BIERCE

AUGUST 11–12

Little drops of water wear down big stones.

~ RUSSIAN PROVERB

AUGUST 13–14

Trees slow of growth bear the best fruit.
~ **Molière**

AUGUST 15–16

The thing that is really hard, and really amazing,
is giving up on being perfect and beginning
the work of becoming yourself.

~ ANNA QUINDLEN

AUGUST 17–18

What wound did ever heal
but by degrees?
~ WILLIAM SHAKESPEARE

AUGUST 19–20

The man who removes a mountain
begins by carrying away small stones.
~ CHINESE PROVERB

AUGUST 21

PATIENCE TIP
Temper Your Temper

A spike in impatience doesn't just fray your nerves. Research shows that the stress hormones it releases also impair cognitive ability, making it more difficult to successfully resolve the situation.

Write a commitment statement below of what you'll do the next time you're down to your last nerve. (HINT: Anything that calms you down—like laughing, singing, or going for a walk—will bring those hormones, and your ability to think clearly, back in line.)

• • •

AUGUST 22

THINK ABOUT . . .
Sticking With It

Researchers have found that grit—
the ability to persevere over long periods
of time to achieve a goal or master a skill—
is a better predictor of success than intelligence.
Think of a time when, despite setbacks, you kept
moving forward to achieve something meaningful.
Write down the details below and let this story
become part of your own personal mythology,
inspiring you whenever you feel
your patience wearing thin.

• • •

AUGUST 23–24

*You get to the point when there are things
you enjoy that start getting hard—
that's when you know you're getting good,
and you have to stick through it.*

~ MICHELLE OBAMA

AUGUST 25–26

*Someone is sitting in the shade today
because someone planted a tree a long time ago.*
~ WARREN BUFFETT

AUGUST 27–28

*An unhurried sense of time is in itself
a form of wealth.*

~ BONNIE FRIEDMAN

AUGUST 29

TRY THIS
Take Patience on the Road

It's easy to get frustrated in the car—
after all, no one can hear you shouting epithets!
But your car can also be a rolling laboratory
for practicing patience. Try blessing anyone
who cuts you off, viewing traffic as a chance
to get engrossed in a podcast, and allowing
others to go first at a four-way stop. When you
see you can still get where you're going
without getting worked up along the way,
you'll be inspired to put those new patience skills
to use in your non-driving life too.

• • •

AUGUST 30–31

Diamonds are nothing more than chunks
of coal that stuck to their jobs.

~ MALCOLM FORBES

SEPTEMBER

Contentment

SEPTEMBER 1

CONTENTMENT TIP
Shun "Should"

There's no joy in acting out of obligation—
it's an uphill trudge with gritted teeth.
If you can't come up with one reason why
you *want* to volunteer as lunch monitor,
sign up for that road race, or visit family,
it's perfectly okay to opt out.

Make a list of the activities you would skip
if the word "should" didn't exist. Allow this list
to encourage you to opt out* any time you feel
pressure to do something you don't wish to do.

*If you have no choice in the matter, find reasons
why that "should" will help you in the long run.

• • •

....

....

....

....

....

....

....

SEPTEMBER 2–3

Be content with what you have;
rejoice in the way things are.
When you realize there is nothing lacking,
the whole world belongs to you.

~ LAO-TZU

....
....
....
....
....

September 4–5

When you come right down to it,
the secret of having it all
is loving it all.

~ Joyce Brothers

....

....

....

....

....

....

September 6–7

*The greater part of our happiness or misery
depends upon our dispositions,
and not upon our circumstances.*

~ Martha Washington

....

....

....

....

....

....

....

SEPTEMBER 8

CONTENTMENT TIP
Loosen Your Grip

Holding on to too much stuff—a basement full of boxes left unopened for years, a closet packed with clothes you don't wear—is at its root motivated by fear: fear that one day you'll need that stuff or that, in giving something away, you'll give up a cherished memory or hurt someone's feelings. If contentment is loving what's happening *right now,* fear is the opposite: It keeps your thoughts on the past or imagining an unhappy future.

What objects can you relinquish? What space in your home can you reclaim from clutter? Go and get rid of whatever just popped into your mind. Loosening your grip on anything that doesn't fill you with joy makes you more available for wonderful developments.

• • •

SEPTEMBER 9–10

*Besides the noble art of getting things done,
there is a nobler art of leaving things undone.*

~ LIN YUTANG

SEPTEMBER 11–12

*If you can't do great things yourself,
remember that you may do
small things in a great way.*

~ NAPOLEON HILL

....

....

....

....

....

....

September 13

TRY THIS
Write Your Own Letter of Acceptance

It's wonderful to want to change and grow.
But disliking who you are today eats up a lot
of energy and prevents progress. To help
embrace the current version of you, make
a list of all the things you forgive yourself for—
whether it's your stretch marks, bank balance,
or forgetfulness. Releasing these judgments
will help you move forward out of love instead
of disgust—the most powerful way to proceed.

• • •

SEPTEMBER 14–15

It is neither wealth nor splendor,
but tranquility and occupation
which give happiness.

~ THOMAS JEFFERSON

....

....

....

....

....

....

....

SEPTEMBER 16–17

We are happy when we are growing.

~ W. B. YEATS

September 18–19

A woman is never sexier than when she's comfortable in her clothes.

~ Vera Wang

....

....

....

....

....

....

SEPTEMBER 20–21

To love what you do and feel that it matters—
how could anything be more fun?

~ KATHARINE GRAHAM

SEPTEMBER 22

CONTENTMENT TIP
Simplify, Simplify, Simplify

Take inspiration from the house cat—inspired
to purr by nothing more than a shaft of light
and a cozy cushion—and make a list
of little things that soothe your soul: the feel
of a warm mug of tea, the sight of a bird visiting
your feeder, the ability of a friend or loved one
to consistently crack you up. When you're
feeling out of sorts, use this list to remind you
of how the littlest things can raise the needle
on your well-being meter.

• • •

SEPTEMBER 23–24

Be grateful for luck. Pay the thunder no mind—
listen to the birds. And don't hate nobody.

~ EUBIE BLAKE

....
....
....
....
....
....
....
....

SEPTEMBER 25–26

Always look at what you have left.
Never look at what you have lost.

~ ROBERT H. SCHULLER

SEPTEMBER 27

THINK ABOUT . . .
Taking Up Space

Think of two houseplants. One grows out
to the very edges of its pot, while the other stays
put in the middle surrounded by plenty of dirt.
Which one would you transplant? That's right,
the one expanding past its present space.

How can you fill up wherever you are today?
If you want a promotion, for example, are you
making the most of your present position?
Fully inhabiting your current position is the
most loving—and gratifying—manner to pave
the way for what's next.

• • •

SEPTEMBER 28

CONTENTMENT TIP
Find Your Sea of Tranquility

According to traditional Chinese medicine,
there is an energy point in the center of your
breastbone known as the Sea of Tranquility.
Pressing this point with your fingers
can deepen your breathing, simultaneously
relaxing and energizing you. The calming
effect it produces is palpable—and magical.

To access it, feel around for a soft spot
on the sternum; it is typically right around
nipple height, directly between your breasts.
Sitting quietly, press this point using one
or two fingertips for at least five breaths
and for as long as feels good. When you notice
your breathing change or your shoulders
unkink, you'll know you've sent a positive
message to your nervous system.

• • •

SEPTEMBER 29–30

You will never be able to escape from your heart.
So it's better to listen to what it has to say.

~ PAULO COELHO

OCTOBER

Wisdom

OCTOBER 1

WISDOM TIP
Stay Curious

Back in March, you learned to observe
your reaction to unexpected events and plant
the seed to accept what happens instead of
feeling angry. The next step in using obstacles
as growth opportunities is to become curious.

When something bad happens, ask yourself:
What good could possibly come from this?
What might this experience teach me?
Staying inquisitive will help you remain
positive and open to growth in every situation,
no matter how challenging.

• • •

OCTOBER 2–3

*Change will only come about when we become
more forgiving, compassionate, loving,
and above all joyful in the knowledge that we can
change as those around us can change too.*

~ MAIREAD MAGUIRE

OCTOBER 4–5

Cease to be a drudge, seek to be an artist.
~ MARY MCLEOD BETHUNE

OCTOBER 6–7

*Be more concerned with your character
than your reputation.*

~ JOHN WOODEN

OCTOBER 8

TRY THIS
Doubt Your Doubts

We're all prone to doubts. Rather than accepting
each doubt as a warning that requires heeding,
use your powers of discernment to question
them. For example, if you think, This will never
work, ask yourself: Really, never? What could
make it more doable? This exercise will help you
stop accepting your doubts as truth and teach
you to look for opportunity instead.

• • •

OCTOBER 9–10

Fall seven times, stand up eight.

~ JAPANESE PROVERB

OCTOBER 11–12

Knowledge does not come to us by details,
but in flashes of light from heaven.
~ HENRY DAVID THOREAU

OCTOBER 13–14

*It is hard to fight an enemy
who has outposts in your head.*

~ SALLY KEMPTON

OCTOBER 15

WISDOM TIP
Be Inspired

Whose example are you thankful for—Helen
Keller, Albert Einstein, your great-aunt Jean?
Write down your list of Chief Inspiration
Officers below. For each, choose qualities they
possess that you'd like to embrace.

To increase their influence, challenge yourself
to learn more about at least one of them in
the next week: Write an inquisitive letter,
invite him or her to tea, read a memoir
or biography. The more you learn about these
figures, the more inspiration they'll provide.

• • •

OCTOBER 16–17

*One must view the world through the eye in one's
heart rather than just trust the eyes in one's head.*

~ MARY CROW DOG

OCTOBER 18–19

Don't compromise yourself.
You are all you've got.

~ JANIS JOPLIN

....
....
....
....
....
....
....

OCTOBER 20–21

Long experience has taught me that
to be criticized is not always to be wrong.

~ ANTHONY EDEN

OCTOBER 22

THINK ABOUT . . .
Don't Force It

It's nice to think we can use our own wisdom
to help others. But unless someone is interested
in receiving help, our good intentions can be
perceived as meddling or, worse, judgment.

If you see a friend or loved one struggling
with something with which you truly feel
you can help, *ask* first. Doing so helps make
someone receptive to what you have to offer,
rather than defensive. If the answer is no, keep
your thoughts to yourself—and avoid gossiping
about the situation with others. Your friends
and family will always remember that you
respected them enough to keep quiet.

• • •

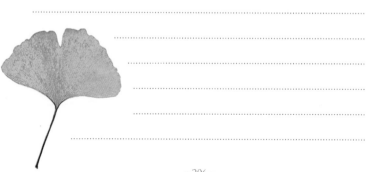

OCTOBER 23–24

Trouble is part of your life, and if you don't share it,
you don't give the person who loves you a chance
to love you enough.

~ DINAH SHORE

....

....

....

....

....

....

....

OCTOBER 25–26

By three methods we may learn wisdom:
First, by reflection, which is noblest; second,
by imitation, which is easiest; and third
by experience, which is the bitterest.

~ CONFUCIUS

October 27–28

The secret of life and art is threefold: getting started, keeping going and getting started again.
~ **Seamus Heaney**

....

....

....

....

....

....

....

OCTOBER 29

TRY THIS
Skip the Drama

We all want to make the best decisions we can,
but agonizing doesn't help. Instead, it tends
to paralyze us with the fear of making a wrong
move. To make better choices in less time,
ask yourself: If it were impossible for me to
make a mistake, what would I do?

This question helps cut through rationaliza-
tions, relieves the need to imagine
all the ways a decision may affect the future, and
taps into your subconscious inner knowledge.

• • •

OCTOBER 30–31

*I don't believe that life is supposed to make you
feel good, or to make you feel miserable either.
Life is just supposed to make you feel.*

~ GLORIA NAYLOR

NOVEMBER

Gratitude

NOVEMBER 1

GRATITUDE TIP
Take Your Wellness Inventory

Below, make four lists titled Mental,
Emotional, Physical, and Spiritual.
Without thinking too hard, write down
all the things you do to take care
of yourself in each area.

Acknowledging your own efforts will help
strengthen your dedication to keep going.
Then, examine the shortest column.
Going forward, what can you do
to boost that area of your life?

• • •

NOVEMBER 2–3

Wake at dawn with winged heart
and give thanks for another day of loving.
~ KAHLIL GIBRAN

November 4–5

*Some people are always grumbling
because roses have thorns;
I am grateful that thorns have roses.*

~ Jean-Baptiste Alphonse Karr

NOVEMBER 6–7

Silent gratitude isn't very much to anyone.

~ GERTRUDE STEIN

NOVEMBER 8

THINK ABOUT . . .
Enjoying the Ride

You've heard the adage before: Life is
a journey, not a destination. But that journey
can feel endless if you don't celebrate the steps
along the way. What long-term projects are you
working toward? What pieces of the process have
you already completed? Write them down
and find a meaningful way to celebrate your
progress thus far: Clink glasses with a friend,
treat yourself to a guilt-free game of Candy
Crush, get a mani-pedi, share a back-patting
status on Twitter. When you recognize
your achievements, your efforts will feel more
like an adventure and less like an arduous trek.

• • •

November 9–10

Gratitude is the memory of the heart.
~ Jean Baptiste Massieu

NOVEMBER 11–12

*Everything has its beauty,
but not everyone sees it.*

~ CONFUCIUS

NOVEMBER 13–14

*We can only be said to be alive in those moments
when our hearts are conscious of our treasures.*

~ THORNTON WILDER

NOVEMBER 15

THINK ABOUT . . .
Embracing Unlikely Teachers

It's an uneasy truth to swallow, but the
fact remains: The people who cause us pain
are also some of our most important teachers.
Think about how a person who's made your life
difficult also taught you a loving lesson.
The emotionally unavailable boyfriend
who dumped you (but taught you what you need
from a partner), the boss who took credit
for your ideas (but helped you learn the value
of self-respect), the friend who betrayed you
(but showed you the importance of your sacred
circle). Write a thank-you note to at least one
of them below, and watch forgiveness bloom.

• • •

NOVEMBER 16–17

When you drink the water, remember the well.

~ **CHINESE PROVERB**

November 18–19

*When we lose one blessing, another is often
and most unexpectedly given in its place.*

~ C. S. Lewis

....

....

....

....

....

....

NOVEMBER 20

TRY THIS
Say It Out Loud

Writing what we're thankful for invites us
to notice the good stuff in our lives.
As powerful as this practice is, however,
it's equally important to open your mouth
and tell those important to you why you're
grateful for them. They will then be more prone
to pass those feelings on to others, creating
a rising tide that lifts many boats. Who do you
want to express your thanks to today?

• • •

November 21–22

Reflect upon your present blessings of which every man has many—not on your past misfortunes, of which all men have some.

~ Charles Dickens

....

....

....

....

....

....

November 23–24

Appreciation is a wonderful thing.
It makes what is excellent in others
belong to us as well.

~ **Voltaire**

....
....
....
....
....
....

November 25–26

The grateful heart sits at a continuous feast.

~ Proverbs 15:15

November 27

GRATITUDE TIP
Appreciate Everything

The power of gratitude kicks into high gear
when you are open to everything that comes
your way, good *and* bad: the cancelled
appointment that gives you unexpected
free time, the fight with your spouse that gets
something unsaid out in the open, the tough
parent-teacher conference that brings
a challenge into clearer focus.

What recent less-than-ideal moments are
you thankful for? Acknowledging the gifts
in everything will help you find ease even
in discomfort—a true recipe for daily calm.

• • •

NOVEMBER 28

GRATITUDE TIP
Let It In

Gratitude goes both ways. The next time
someone says "Thank you" or pays you
a compliment, let the sentiment penetrate.
Resist the urge to say anything right away—
no deflecting the compliment or brushing it off.
Simply let the sentiment warm your heart
for a moment; a simple "You're welcome"
or "That means a lot to me" will do.
Learning to accept moments of recognition
will help you feel more appreciated by the
most important person of all: yourself.

• • •

November 29–30

Take as a gift whatever the day brings forth.

~ Horace